A
CONTRACT
WITH
GOD

The Will Eisner Library

from W.W. Norton & Company

Hardcover Compilations

The Contract with God Trilogy: Life on Dropsie Avenue
Will Eisner's New York
Brush Strokes: My Life in Pictures

Paperbacks

A Contract With God
A Life Force
New York: The Big City
City People Notebook
Will Eisner Reader
The Dreamer
Invisible People
To the Heart of the Storm
Dropsie Avenue
Life on Another Planet
A Family Matter
Minor Miracles
The Name of the Game
The Building
The Plot: The Secret Story of the Protocols of the Elders of Zion

Other Graphic Novels by Will Eisner

Fagin the Jew
Last Day in Vietnam

A Contract With God

and Other Tenement Stories

A Graphic Novel by

Will Eisner

W. W. Norton & Company
New York • London

Printed in the United States of America
First published as a Norton paperback 2006

Manufacturing by LSC Communications, Willard Division
Production: Julia Druskin and Sue Carlson

The Library of Congress has cataloged the one-volume edition as follows:
Eisner, Will.
The contract with God trilogy : life on Dropsie Avenue / Will Eisner.
p. cm.
Contents: A contract with God—A life force—Dropsie Avenue.
ISBN 0-393-06105-1
1. Graphic Novels. I. Title: Life on Dropsie Avenue. II. Eisner, Will. Contract with God.
III. Eisner, Will. Life force. IV. Eisner, Will. Dropsie Avenue. V. Title

PN6727.E4A6 2005
741.5'973—dc33
2005053944

ISBN-13: 978-0-393-32804-2 pbk.
ISBN-10: 0-393-32804-X pbk.

W. W. Norton & Company, Inc., 500 Fifth Avenue, New York, N.Y. 10110
www.wwnorton.com

W. W. Norton & Company Ltd., 15 Carlisle Street, London W1D 3BS

8 9 0

Contents

List of New Illustrations

55

Preface

This book contains stories drawn from the endless flow of happenings characteristic of city life. Some are true. Some could be true.

Born and brought up in New York City and having survived and thrived there, I carry with me a cargo of memories, some painful and some pleasant, which have remained locked in the hold of my mind. I have an ancient mariner's need to share my accumulation of experience and observations. Call me, if you will, a graphic witness reporting on life, death, heartbreak and the never-ending struggle to prevail . . . or at least to survive.

In 1978, encouraged by the work of the experimental graphic artists Otto Nückel, Franz Masareel and Lynd Ward, who in the 1930s published serious novels told in art without text, I attempted a major work in a similar form. In a futile effort to entice the patronage of a mainstream publisher, I called it a "graphic novel." It was a collection of four related stories, drawn from memory, which took place in a single tenement in the Bronx. The title of the book, named for the lead story, became *A Contract With God.* Though no major publisher would touch it at the time, this novel has remained in print for twenty-seven years, and has been published in eleven different languages. I followed this first effort with other more ambitiously constructed graphic novels. All are anchored on a single street in the borough of the Bronx in New York City. The street is Dropsie Avenue, a caricature of a neighborhood that is nevertheless very real to me.

As the story unfolds, it is at 55 Dropsie Avenue where Frimme Hersh deals with God; where the street singer fails to grasp his chance for glory. It is on Dropsie Avenue where a diminutive enemy defeats the super, and Willie comes of age. It is also on Dropsie Avenue, finally, where I undertake the biography of the street itself, through the physical evolution of the block, the rise and fall of the tenement building at No. 55 and the ethnic and social changes of its stream of occupants.

The tenement—the name derives from a fifteenth-

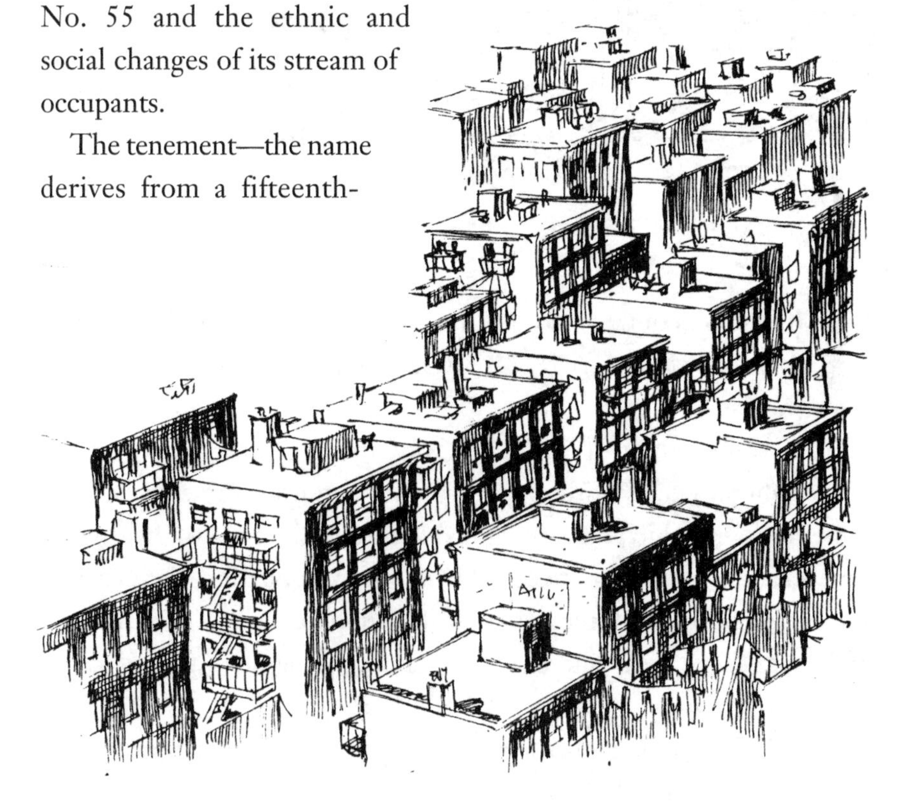

century legal term for a multiple dwelling—always seemed to me a "ship afloat in concrete." After all, didn't the building carry its passengers on a voyage through life? No. 55 sat at the corner of Dropsie Avenue near the elevated train, or the elevated as we called it in those days. It was a treasure house of stories that illustrated tenement life as I remembered it, stories that needed to be told before they faded from memory. Within its "railroad flats," with rooms strung together train-like, lived low-paid city employees or laborers and their turbulent families. Most were recent immigrants, intent on their own survival. They kept busy raising children and dreaming of the better life they knew existed "uptown." Hallways were filled with a rich stew of cooking aromas, sounds of arguments, and the tinny wail from Victrolas. What community spirit there was stemmed from the common hostility of tenants toward the landlord or his surrogate superintendent. Typically, the building's tenants came and went with regularity, depending on the vagaries of their fortunes. But many remained for a lifetime, imprisoned there by poverty or old age. Within its walls great dramas played out. There was no real privacy or anonymity. Everybody knew about everybody. Human dramas, both good and bad, instantly gathered witnesses like ants swarming around a piece of dropped food. From window to window or on the stoop below, the tenants analyzed, evaluated and critiqued each happening, following an obligatory admission that it was really none of their business.

"A Contract With God," the first part of this book, examines the subject of man's relationship with his God. This very basic human preoccupation stems from the primal concern with survival. We are told early on that God will either punish us or reward us, depending on our behavior, in accordance with a compact. The clergy provides the terms, edicts, and conditions, and our parents enforce this contract.

The creation of this story was an exercise in personal agony. My only daughter, Alice, had died of leukemia eight years before the publication of this book. My grief was still raw. My heart still bled. In fact, I could not even then bring myself to discuss the loss. I made Frimme Hersh's daughter an "adopted child." But his anguish was mine. His argument with God was also mine. I exorcised my rage at a deity that I believed violated my faith and deprived my lovely 16-year-old child of her life at the very flowering of it. This is the first time in thirty-four years that I have openly discussed it.

"The Street Singer" was a creature of the Depression years. These were desperate times when no device to earn some money was beyond reproach. The street singers were men who appeared in the narrow space between the tenements to provide impromptu concerts. As a boy I often tossed a penny down into our back alley for the man who regularly appeared there to sing, in a wine-soaked voice, popular songs or off-key operatic arias. Mothers seemed charmed by this seedy romantic troubadour. Fathers were sure he was a spy for robbers, and the meaner kids sometimes threw down a button wrapped in paper to see how angry the man would get when he opened it. To me, however, he brought a bit of theatrical glamour to the grim alley. The mystery about who he was has remained with me over the years. Finally, with this book about tenement life, I was able to immortalize his story.

"The Super" is a story built around the mysterious but threatening custodian of the Bronx apartment house where I lived as a young boy. Since we never had contact with or even knew the landlord, the superintendent was the person we dealt with on the day-to-day matters of habitation. He lived in the cellar, was unmarried, and seemed perpetually cranky, probably because he was constantly being annoyed by tenants who demanded repairs, better heat in the winter, or complained about poor maintenance. Generally the super was feared and avoided, and blamed for any unusual happening, real or imagined.

"Cookalein," the final story in the book, is a Yiddish-English word, which means "cook alone." It describes a summer resort on a farm where the guests cooked their own meals. Each summer, in the Catskill Mountains about 150 miles from New York City, not far from the more upscale resorts that catered to the urban middle class, farmers made some extra money by opening their farms to vacationers. Many farmers built small "bungalows," forerunners to the motels of the '40s, on their properties. They opened their kitchens in the "main house" for mothers to cook meals for their families. A rental was very cheap. No maid service or food was included, and guests brought their own linens. The countryside excursion was a welcome experience, particularly for the young, who had a chance to help with farm chores, watch the process of animal life, drink milk from cows' udders and, most crucially, enjoy the freedom of living away from the prison-like environment of the city. In this brief exposure to a bucolic atmosphere, a young boy, amid the drama of his parents' lives, could have his first romance and a first real sexual experience—an ethereal event—in the clear air and wholesomeness of a mountain farm. Glamour and excitement, which wafted down from the great

hotels only a few miles away, added to the theatrics of the summer holiday. "Cookalein" is a combination of invention and recall. It is an honest account of my coming of age.

I've spent a long career—spanning eight decades—combining and refining words and pictures. My early work in newspaper comics and comic books allowed me to entertain millions of readers weekly, but I always felt there was more to say. I pioneered the use of comics for instructional manuals for American soldiers, covering three major wars, and later used comics to educate grade school children. Both were heady responsibilities that I took very seriously. But I yearned to do still more with the medium. At an age when I could have "retired," I chose instead to create literary comics, then a decidedly oxymoronic term. Acceptance has not always been easy, but I have seen it arrive in my lifetime. It has been most gratifying to see the graphic novel and many of its exceptional creators gradually become an accepted part of the book world. I couldn't find a major publisher to take *A Contract With God* only a quarter century ago, and now graphic novels represent the book industry's fastest growing genre.

This graphic novel represents a vital part of my *oeuvre*. It brings great satisfaction to know that it will now reach a new generation of readers.

Will Eisner

Tamarac, Florida
December 2004

Preface to the 2000 Edition

Early in 1940, after an intimate involvement with the birth and burgeoning of the so-called comic book art form, I undertook a weekly series entitled *The Spirit*. This was to be a complete story to appear as a newspaper insert comic book every Sunday. It revolved around a freelance masked crime fighter in the heroic tradition and would, the distributing syndicate hoped, latch on to the growing national interest in comic books.

With all the self-assurance of youth, I plunged into the task without much real planning. It was not until I came up for air after the first fifteen weeks that I realized the full magnitude of this undertaking. In fact, I was delivering a short story a week to an audience far more sophisticated and demanding than the newsstand comic book reader. The reality of the task and the enormous perimeters of the opportunity were thrilling, and I responded with the euphoria and enthusiasm of a frontiersman. In the twelve years that followed, I thrashed out this virgin territory in an orgy of experiment, using *The Spirit* as the launching platform for all the ideas that swam in my head.

With hindsight, I realize I was really only working around one core concept—that the medium, the arrangement of words and pictures in a sequence—was an art form in itself. Unique, with a structure and gestalt all its own, this medium could deal with meaningful themes. Certainly there was more for the cartoonist working in this technique to deal with than superheroes who were preventing the destruction of Earth by supervillains.

I was not alone in this belief. In the middle of the 1930s, Lynd Ward explored this path in his remarkable attempts at graphic storytelling. He produced several complete novels in woodcuts. One of these books, *Frankenstein*, fell into my hands in 1938 and it had an influence on my thinking thereafter. I consider my efforts in this area attempts at expansion or extension of Ward's original premise.

At the time, to openly discuss comics as an art form—or indeed to claim any autonomy or legitimacy for them—was considered a gross presumption worthy only of ridicule. In the intervening years, however, recognition and acceptance had fertilized the soil, and sequential art stands at the threshold of joining the cultural establishment. Now, in this climate warmed by serious adult attention, creators can attempt new growth in a field that formerly yielded only what Jules Feiffer referred to as junk art. The proliferation of stunning art and imaginative exploration is but an early harvest of this germination. For me, the years after I stopped producing *The Spirit* were devoted to the application of the comic book art form to education, instruction, and other pragmatic directions. Satisfying and rewarding as these were, they were also demanding, and so there was little time available to pursue the experiments I set aside in 1951. Twenty-five years later, given the time and opportunity, I embarked on the effort which you hold in your hands; a harvest at last from seedlings I had carried around with me all those years.

In this book, I have attempted to create a narrative that deals with intimate themes. In the four stories, housed in a tenement, I undertook to draw on memory culled from my own experiences and that of my contemporaries. I have tried to tell how it was in a corner of America that is still to be revisited.

The people and events in these narratives, while compounded from recall, are things which I would have you accept as real. Obviously in the creation, names and faces were rearranged. It is important to understand the times and the place in which these stories are set. Fundamentally, they were not unlike the way the world of today is for those who live in crowded proximity and in depersonalized housing. The importance of dealing with the ebb and flow of city existence and the overriding effort to escape it never seems to change for the inhabitants.

In the telling of these stories, I tried to adhere to a rule of realism which requires that caricature or exaggeration accept the limitations of actuality. To accomplish a sense of dimension, I set aside two basic working constrictions that so often inhibit the medium—space and format. Accordingly, each story was written without regard to space, and each was allowed to develop its format from itself; that is, to evolve from the narration. The normal frames (or panels) associated with sequential (comic book) art are allowed to take on their integrity. For example, in many cases an entire page is set out as a panel. The text and the balloons are interlocked with the art. I see all these as threads of a single fabric and exploit them as a language. If I have been successful at this, there will be no interruption in the flow of narrative because the picture and the text are so totally dependent on each other as to be inseparable for even a moment.

Finally, I must confess to a certain sense of uneasiness at trying to explain what I'm about to present. I have always cringed with embarrassment when listening to an artist, writer, or musician preamble an offering with an explanation of what he or she is trying to do. It is almost as though one is begging the audience to excuse the imperfections or—at the very best—seeking to influence the judgment that will surely come. Perhaps I, too, am a victim of this insecurity, because for me, this is a new path in the forest.

To colleagues who encouraged the effort, to my family who urged me to try, to Rose Kaplan, who edited this work, and the others who read the early drafts and offered advice—my thanks.

White Plains, New York
August 1978

Addendum to the third printing: In the years since *A Contract With God* was first published, the book has been translated into six languages, including, appropriately, Yiddish—a language in which I can think but cannot read or write. I have since written several books in this medium. They are more polished technically but with this maiden work, a big piece of my heart remains.

Tamarac, Florida
January 1989

Addendum to the fifth printing: In the seventeen years that *A Contract With God* has remained in print, the enlarging field of fine graphic novels has reinforced my belief that there would be a continually growing audience for the literary pretensions of this medium. After many subsequent works, I can still look back at this maiden effort without embarrassment and I retain for it the special affection one has for a first child.

Tamarac, Florida
June 1995

Addendum to the DC Edition first printing: Now, at long last this book, my first graphic novel, will enter its seventh printing under the DC Comics flag. After 22 years of being "in print" it is assuring to know that its future will be in their strong and knowledgeable hands.

I want also to acknowledge my deep gratitude to Denis Kitchen, who was responsible for its continued publication during most of those years.

Will Eisner

Tamarac, Florida
March 2000

A TENEMENT IN THE BRONX

At 55 Dropsie Avenue, the Bronx, New York– not far from the elevated station– stood the tenement.

Like the others, it was built around 1920 when the decaying apartment houses in lower Manhattan could no longer accommodate the flood of immigrants that poured into New York after World War I.

These buildings – called "Tenements" after the 16th century legal term for a multiple dwelling that housed tenants – soon occupied large tracts of Bronx land.

By 1930 they were already part of the roots of a whole new group of first-generation Americans and their foreign-born parents.

Inside – in the "railroad-flat" layouts lived low-paid city employees, laborers, clerks and their families. They teemed with a noisy neighborliness not unlike the life-style the newcomers had left on the "other side." It was a kind of ship board fellowship of passengers in transit—for, they were on a voyage of upward mobility.

They were intent on their own survival, busy with breeding their young and dreaming of a better life they knew existed "Uptown."

What community spirit there was, stemmed from their hostility toward a common enemy—the landlord!

55 Dropsie Avenue was typical of most tenements. Its tenants were varied. Some came and went. Many remained there for a life time... imprisoned by poverty or other factors. It was a sort of micro-village—and the world was **Dropsie Avenue**.

Within its walls
great dramas were
played out.
There was no real
privacy-no anonymity.
One was either a
participant or a
member of the
front-row audience.
"Everybody
knew about
everybody."
The following
stories are based
on life in these
tenements during
the 1930's...the
dirty thirties!
They are true
stories.
Only the telling
and the
portrayals have
converted
them to fiction.
Will Eisner

1

A
CONTRACT
WITH
GOD

All day the rain poured down on the Bronx without mercy.

The sewers overflowed and the waters rose over the curbs of the street.

The tenement at No.55 Dropsie Avenue seemed ready to rise and float away on the swirling tide. "Like the ark of Noah," it seemed to Frimme Hersh as he sloshed homeward.

Only the tears of
ten thousand
weeping angels
could cause
such a deluge!
And, come to think
of it, maybe
that is exactly
what it was...

...after all, this was the day Frimme Hersh buried Rachele, his daughter.

Not so unusual,
a father brings
up a child with
care and love
only to lose her
... plucked, as it
were, from his
arms by an
unseen hand
-the hand of GOD.
It happens to
lots of people
every day.

...to others, maybe.

... but not to Frimme Hersh.

And why not to Frimme Hersh ??

That's a fair question!

It should not have happened to Frimme Hersh

BECAUSE FRIMME HERSH HAD A CONTRACT WITH GOD!

And
a contract
is a
contract!
It was, after
all, a solemn
agreement of
many years.

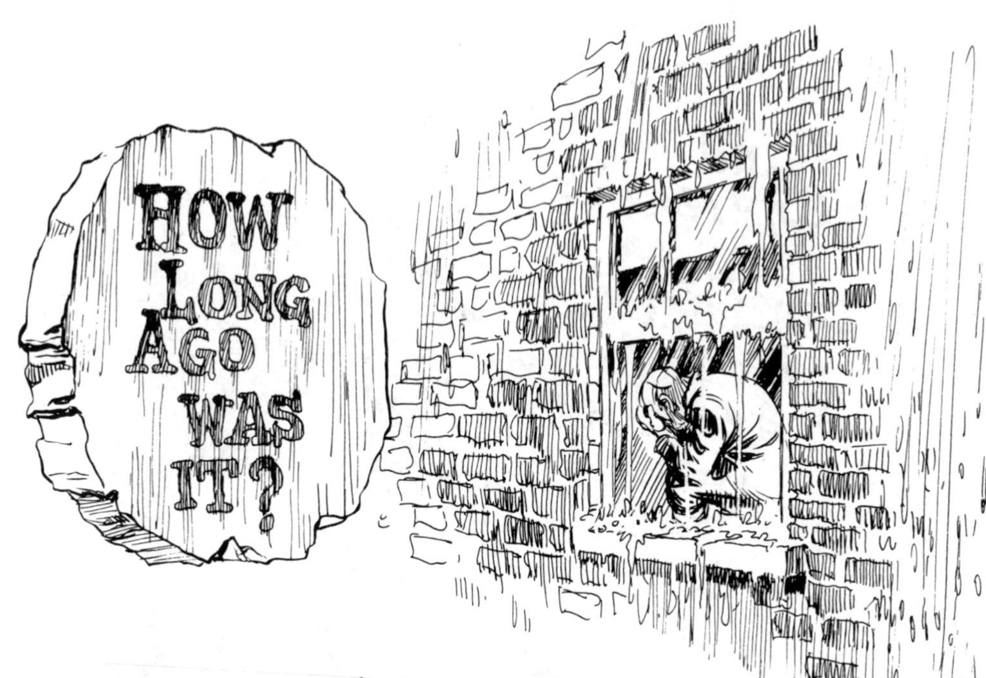

In 1881 Tsar Alexander II of Russia was assassinated and a wave of terrible anti-semitic pogroms swept the country.

In that year also, Frimme Hersh was born in a little village near Tiflis, named Piske.

Somehow his family survived the massacre and Frimmehleh, as he was lovingly called, grew up.

By the time he was ten, it became clear that this boy was special. He was brilliant and seemed to acquire knowledge from the air. In a poor shtetl like Piske, where survival was the main concern, how else?

Above all, Frimmehleh was helpful and kind. After his parents died, he became the child of the childless in Piske.
THANK YOU FOR YOUR KINDNESS, FRIMMEHLEH.
GOD WILL REWARD YOU.

In those years, this was said to him often for he performed many, many good deeds.

One day, after a terrible attack, the surviving elders summoned him.

...And so Hersh obeyed. Two nights later on the trail deep in the forest...

THEN I WILL MAKE A CONTRACT WITH GOD!
And that night in the cold forest, he wrote the contract on a small stone.

And with the little stone tablet in his pocket, Frimme Hersh settled in New York City where he found shelter in the Hassidic community. There he took religious instruction and devoted himself to good works.

Faithfully and piously, he adhered to the terms of his contract with GOD.

In time he became a respected member of the Synagogue, trusted with money and social matters. So it was not surprising that it was on Hersh's doorstep that an anonymous mother abandoned her infant girl. What could be clearer? To Frimme, this was part of his pact with GOD.

Since no one wanted a child born of GOD-Knows-What Kind of parents, Frimme Hersh adopted the baby himself. He named her Rachele, after his mother, and devoted himself to her with all his love.

So, she grew up blossoming in the warmth and nourishment of Frimme's gentle heart and pious ways. She was indeed his child and the joy of his years. Then one day– in the springtime of her life–Rachele fell ill.

Suddenly and fatally.

NO!
NOT TO ME... YOU CAN'T DO THIS... WE HAVE A CONTRACT !!

That night Frimme Hersh confronted GOD...

...and the old tenement trembled under the fury of the dialogue.

IF GOD REQUIRES THAT MEN HONOR THEIR AGREEMENTS...
...THEN IS NOT GOD, ALSO, SO OBLIGATED ??

I ASK YOU...WERE THE TERMS NOT CLEARLY WRITTEN ??
...DID I IGNORE EVEN ONE TINY SENTENCE - OR PERHAPS A SINGLE COMMA ?

ENOUGH.

CLANK

All during the days of mourning that followed the funeral, the rain fell without pause.
Friends came-each offering Hersh the usual words of comfort which he accepted in stony silence.

At the end of the days of Shiva in the dawn of the eighth day, the sun rose in a clear sky and Frimme Hersh said the morning prayer...for the last time.

Then... with deliberation.... he shaved off his beard...

WELL, NOW... IT'S AN EXPENSIVE PIECE OF PROPERTY.
WHAT E-X-P-E-N-S-I-V-E? PLEASE, MR. JOHNSON, I KNOW YOU FORECLOSED ON IT TWICE!

SO, FOR THE MORTGAGE I'LL BUY IT!... BELIEVE ME, IT AIN'T WORTH IT... BUT IT'S A START!
HMPFF... WELL, NOW, I THINK WE CAN MAKE A DEAL! ... WHAT IS YOUR FINANCIAL WORTH?

BONDS, I GOT- NO CASH... SO CAN YOU LOAN ME ON THESE?
THEY'LL DO FINE... AMPLE EQUITY THERE. - MR. HERSH, WE HAVE A DEAL!

For the first time, Frimme HersH lied. For the first time, he committed an act which formerly was unthinkable. The bonds were not his- they had only been entrusted to him for safekeeping by the synagogue.
BANK
...SO, WHAT WAS SO HARD ABOUT THAT? ...HA! WHAT A YOLD!
...AND BESIDES, WHO AM I HURTING?! IN A YEAR I'LL BUY BACK THE BONDS... SO, A BIG TSIMMES!!

So, Frimme Hersh became the new owner of 55 Dropsie Avenue.

YOU WILL ALSO CUT DOWN ON STEAM HEAT 10%. FROM NOW ON THE TENANTS WILL MAKE THEIR OWN REPAIRS... I DON'T WANT TO KNOW FROM NO COMPLAINTS!
ACH... THESE JEWS ...YESTERDAY A POOR TENANT, TODAY THE OWNER! ...HOW DO THEY DO IT ?!

Within a year, Frimme Hersh gleaned enough out of the property to acquire the one next door. Within the next three years, he accumulated the beginning of a real estate empire.

His success appeared to be as much the result of uncanny luck as anything else.

Before long he took a mistress, a 'Shikseh' from Scranton, Pa., and took up a lifestyle he felt more appropriate to his new station.

He traded buildings like toys.

But one building he never sold - the tenement on Dropsie Ave. At least once every week he would come there... just to look at it.

WHY DON'T YOU SELL THOSE CRUMMY BUILDINGS, FRIM?!
WHY DON'T YOU MIND YOUR OWN BUSINESS!!
Y'KNOW, FRIM, YOU GOT, LIKE, A BLACK HOLE INSIDE O' YOU!
YOU DON'T DRINK... YEAH, THAT'S IT-HAVE A DRINK! MY FATHER USED TO SAY IT FILLED THE BLACK HOLE INSIDE HIM... COME ON, BABY, TRY IT!

TRY... COME ON.
AAAH.. Y'R HOPELESS!
...WE NEVER GO NOWHERE, FRIM! WHAT KIND OF LIFE IS THIS?– YOU'RE SO RICH YOU CAN BUY ANYTHING YOU WANT... SO, BUY IT!!
WE DON'T EVEN GO TO NO CHURCH...

HEY! Y'WANT I SHOULD BECOME JEWISH ?
FRIM? FRIM? NOW, WHAT DID I SAY WRONG ?

One evening Frimme Hersh walked from his penthouse uptown all the way to the old Synagogue.

A FEW YEARS AGO I USED THE CONGREGATION'S BONDS AS COLLATERAL. NOW I CAN REPAY YOU.

SO, I'M RETURNING THEM, WITH INTEREST!
WE ARE ALL GRATEFUL.

NOW, I NEED SOMETHING FROM YOU!
FROM US? ...WHAT CAN WE GIVE A WEALTHY MAN?

Carefully, Hersh recounted the history of his former contract.

THAT CONTRACT WAS WRITTEN WHEN I WAS A CHILD-SO, WHO KNOWS, MAYBE IT WAS POORLY WRITTEN !
BUT MR. HERSH, THIS IS A PRIVATE MATTER BETWEEN YOU AND GOD !!
YOU ARE LEARNED IN THE WORD OF GOD -AND IF YOU KNOW HIS WORD YOU KNOW HIS WILL !

And so the three old men pondered the request.

BUT, REBBE, WOULD IT NOT BE A BLASPHEMY IF WE SHOULD **DEVIATE** FROM THE LAW?
WE WILL NOT DEVIATE! ...WE WILL **ABBREVIATE**!

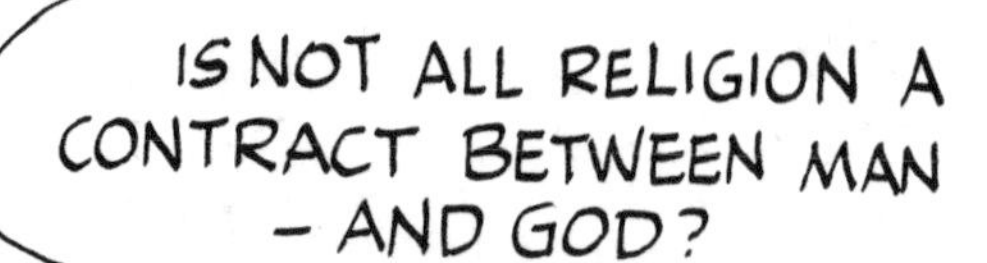
IS NOT ALL RELIGION A CONTRACT BETWEEN MAN - AND GOD?

SO, WHAT IS HERSH ASKING FOR, AFTER ALL??...HE IS ASKING US TO PROVIDE HIM WITH A GUIDING DOCUMENT-SO THAT HE MIGHT LIVE IN HARMONY WITH GOD... CAN WE TRULY DENY HIM THIS??

So in the days that followed, the elders toiled, interrupted only by the Sabbath and certain days of prayer. At last they presented the document to Hersh.
-YES... YES...YES AHA YES, YES!
AND NOW, I WILL LIVE UP TO MY BARGAIN-HERE IS THE LEASE TO THE TENEMENT-IN THE NAME OF THE SYNAGOGUE.
FRIMME HERSH, YOU ARE A MAN OF YOUR WORD!

All that night Hersh sat reading the contract. Again and again... he studied every word with great care.

AT LAST-I HAVE A GENUINE CONTRACT WITH GOD!

I WILL MAKE A NEW LIFE. I WILL GIVE ... I WILL DO CHARITABLE WORK AGAIN...

... AND, AND AFTER ALL - I AM NOT TOO OLD TO MARRY. I SHALL HAVE A DAUGHTER... AND I SHALL NAME HER RACHELE, YES, YES !!

THIS TIME, YOU WILL NOT VIOLATE OUR CONTRACT !
THIS TIME, I HAVE THREE WITNESSES!
THIS TIME I
ULP MY CHEST A PAIN IN
GLAK!

At the exact moment of Hersh's last earthly breath... a mighty bolt of lightning struck the city... Not a drop of rain fell.... Only an angry wind swirled about the tenements.

On Dropsie Avenue the old tenements seemed to tremble in the storm. It reminded the tenants of that day, years ago, when Frimme Hersh argued with GOD and terminated their contract.

REAL ESTATE TYCOON DIES

HEAD OF REALTY CO EMPIRE

EPILOGUE

Around midnight, fires started on the roof of a Dropsie Avenue tenement. Soon the flames, spreading quickly, consumed all the old buildings on the street.
All.... except one! Miraculously the tenement at 55 Dropsie Avenue was unharmed.

And it happened that a boy,
Shloime Khreks, was
the hero of the day.

Shloime was a New Boy ..... And because he was so different, he became the object of much bullying. One day, not long after the fire, he was trapped in the alley of Number 55 by three toughs.

HEY MOIF..., LOOK, IT'S THE NEW KID! LET'S GIVE HIM A NICE E-NEE-SHE-AY-SHUN.
THAT'S SHLOIME KHREKS, HE'S A HASSID-HAW!
HE WEARS A FUNNY HAT!
LET'S GET OUTTA HERE.
HEY LOOK OUT HE'S FIGHTIN' BACK!
HE'S THROWIN ROCKS BACK AT US... OWCH

...THERE IS WRITING ON THIS STONE.

IT'S A CONTRACT
A...A CONTRACT WITH GOD!

I WILL KEEP IT!

...And that evening on the stoop of the tenement, Shloime Khreks signed his name below that of Frimme Hersh... thereby entering into a contract with GOD.

2

THE STREET SINGER
During the early 1930s, at the depth of the Great Depression, there appeared in the alleys of the tenements, STREET SINGERS.
These wandering street minstrels sang popular songs and segments of operatic arias which in the acoustics of the place, sounded surprisingly professional.

On warm Summer afternoons these victims of the hard times entertained their unseen audience who rewarded their efforts....

No one knew much about them...

MILANO

KNOCK
KNOCK
YES...
I'M COMING
I'M COMING

YOUR NOTE-IT SAID FOR ME TO COME UP?!
YES...YES, COME IN...

...DO COME IN, PLEASE! OH, WE HAVE SO MUCH TO TALK ABOUT.

YOU KNOW, YOU HAVE A GOLDEN VOICE - HAVE YOU EVER CONSIDERED A PROFESSIONAL CAREER?

HAVE YOU EVER HEARD OF **DIVA MARTA MARIA** THE SOPRANO?
YOU GOT SOMETHING TO EAT? THIS FRUIT IS WAX!
I...AM... DIVA MARTA MARIA !!

I TRAINED WITH THE GREAT MADAME LA SHTIMME... OF COURSE YOU HEARD OF HER!?
PASS THE SALT.

FOR YEARS I SANG IN CONCERT HALLS AND WITH OPERA COMPANIES ALL OVER THE WORLD...

...THEN, I MARRIED !!

MY HUSBAND WAS A DRUNKARD- HE BEAT ME! HE WAS INSANELY JEALOUS... OFTEN HE WAS SICK! I STOPPED SINGING AND GAVE LESSONS SO I COULD TAKE CARE OF HIM.

FINALLY... IN HOBOKEN ONE WINTER HE DIED – AT LAST!

FIRST... WHAT IS YOUR NAME??... OH, NEVER MIND, I'LL GIVE YOU A NEW NAME. HMMM, LET ME SEE...

RONALD BARRY!!! YES, THAT'S IT, YOU'LL BE RONALD BARRY THE GOLDEN BARITONE!

YOU LOOK LIKE QUALITY! Y'KNOW, YOU RESEMBLE JOHN BARRYMORE. HMMM, NO... MORE LIKE RONALD COLMAN! YOU ARE VERY ATTRACTIVE... WITH YOUR VOICE AND LOOKS-AND MY EXPERIENCE... WE'LL MAKE IT TO THE TOP-TOGETHER!!
RIALTO

AND YOU'LL BE MY LOVER....

...TOGETHER WE WILL CREATE THE GOLDEN BARITONE...
... ANOTHER 'SHEIK OF ARABY' YOU WILL BE A STAR... OH GOD A STAR.

YOU'LL SEE... IT WILL ALWAYS BE LIKE THIS.

AND NOW, MY DEAR, WE MUST START ON OUR CAREER- YOU WILL NEED MANY THINGS... CLOTHES, VOICE LESSONS, BOOKINGS!

HERE IS SOME MONEY – BUY YOURSELF A NEW SUIT! IN THIS BUSINESS YOU MUST LOOK PROSPEROUS!

TOMORROW YOU'LL BEGIN SINGING LESSONS - WITH **ME**!

COME BACK TOMORROW AT NINE O'CLOCK ... WE START IN THE MORNING EARLY ... OH, IT WILL BE HARD WORK, A LOT OF DISCIPLINE AND I SHALL BE A HARD TASKMASTER!

– UNTIL TOMORROW MORNING THEN ... ♫RONALD♫

SO MUCH TO DO

HELLO, MAX? THIS IS MARTA MARIA...
-OH YOU KNOW WHO...THAT'S MY STAGE NAME, REMEMBER? IT'S SYLVIA... SYLVIA SPEEGEL!

WAIT-DON'T HANG UP!!!

LISTEN, I HAVE A NEW PROTEGE... A GOLDEN BARITONE, RONALD BARRY - OF COURSE YOU NEVER HEARD OF HIM-BUT YOU WILL!

I'M GOING TO COACH HIM-MAX, GET HIM A BOOKING...A START, ANYWHERE-WEDDINGS, A BAR MITZVAH-A WAKE, ANYTHING...MAX, DON'T TALK DIRTY, HE'S MY PROTEGE...PLEASE, SO MUCH DEPENDS ON THIS... ...MAX...MAX...

MAX ... I'M BEGGING MAX ... PLEASE

... YOU'LL DO IT? .. OH, **GOD BLESS YOU** MAX ... THANK YOU ... I ... HELLO HELLO

AT LAST
WE ARE GOING TO BE ON TOP AGAIN!
HELD OVER

HEY, JOE... IT'S ME, EDDIE!
YOU AGAIN?
KNOCK KNOCK

HERE Y'ARE. Y'GOT MONEY THIS TIME?
PLENTY!

WAAHH

WAHHH
WAHH

WAHHHH
SO, EDDIE, YOU BUM, YER HOME EARLY...'SMATTER, YER VOICE GAVE OUT? ...I HOPE!

WAAA
ALL THAT WHISKEY WOULD KILL A HORSE! EDDIE, Y'GONNA DRINK YERSELF INTO THE GRAVE!
WAAAAAAA
SHADDAP! SHET THAT KID'S MOUTH!!
EEE
WAAAHH

YOU'LL KILL MY BABY! -MURDERER!! DRUNKARD!
SHADDAP
WHERE'D YOU GET THE MONEY FOR ALL THAT WHISKEY... I NEED MONEY FOR THE DOCTOR... YOU KNOW I'M PREGNANT.
SHADDAP
HMPF... IS THIS ALL?? YOU SPEND 20 DOLLARS ON WHISKEY AND YOU GIVE ME ONLY 5 BUCKS- HOW CAN WE LIVE ON THIS ?!
SHADDAP

LOOK AT ME...I WAS SUCH A BEAUTIFUL DANCER... I GAVE UP A CAREER TO MARRY AN ACCOUNTANT!
SHADDAP

BUT NO... HE DON'T WANT A STEADY JOB -HE'D RATHER SING IN STINKIN' ALLEYS FOR PENNIES.
SHADDAP!

YOU DON'T EVEN KNOW HOW TO SING
YOU DIDN'T EVEN WHISTLE BEFORE YOU MET ME!

SHADDAP

BUM BUM
SHADDAP

HALP HE'S KILLING ME AND MY BABY
SHADDAP SHADDAP SHADDAP SHADDAP
WAH
WAHH
WAH WAH
I'M GOIN' TO BED..
...YOU BROKE MY BOTTLE...

EDDIE...IT'S NOON ALREADY-PLEASE, GO OUT AND LOOK FOR A JOB.... PLEASE!

I'M SORRY ABOUT LAST NIGHT, SOPHIE.
THAT'S OKAY, EDDIE! GO, HONEY... DON'T SING TODAY-GET A JOB!

JOE, GIMME A HAIR-OF-THE-DOG ::COUGH:: HAD A ROUGH NIGHT.
BEAT IT, EDDIE! Y'R CREDIT STINKS.

ONLY TEMPORARILY! JOE, YOU ARE LOOKING AT THE NEW PROTEGE OF THE GREAT DIVA MARTA MARIA - THE INTERNATIONALLY FAMOUS SOPRANO!
DIVA WHO ?

WHAT DO YOU KNOW ABOUT THE WORLD OF MUSIC..?!

IT'S THE BIG TIME... LOTS OF MONEY... RESPECT, TRAVEL - THE BIG TIME, JOE! NOTHIN' BUT THE BEST!
WHY IS THIS DIVA GONNA DO ALL THIS FOR YOU ?

Y'SEE... MY PLAN IS LET HER PROMOTE ME ...THEN WHEN I'M ONTOP–I'LL GO BACK TO MY WIFE AND KID... A SINGING STAR... NOT A CRUMMY ACCOUNTANT.

I...DON'T KNOW WHERE... I DIDN'T THINK TO WRITE DOWN THE ADDRESS! I SING IN SO MANY ALLEYS -THEY ALL **LOOK** ALIKE !
NO..NO... WAIT-I'LL SHOW YOU- SHE MUST BE IN THE PHONE BOOK!
NOTHING... SHE'S NOT LISTED.
YOU CONNED ME OUTTA A DRINK AGAIN!
JOE... SHE REALLY.. ...I'M NOT LYING...
GET OUT!

OUT!
JOE'S

Street Singers played a tenement only once.
There were, after all, plenty of alleys...

3

The SUPER
SUPER
The tenement was like a passenger ship anchored in a sea of concrete. In its bowels lived the Captain. He was called the SUPER.

The super at 55 Dropsie was Mr. Scuggs.
MISTER SCUGGS, WHEN YOU GONNA FIX THE HALL STEPS? WHAT KINDA BUILDING YOU RUNNIN' HA??
Nobody really liked Mr. Scuggs.

I'M RUNNING THIS BUILDING MR. LEVINSKY! AND I'LL DECIDE WHEN THINGS NEED TO BE FIXED!
Infact, they were a little afraid of him...why, who knows?

Perhaps it was what they **didn't** know that fed the fear.

YAH!... BACK IN CHERMANY THINGS IS DIFFERENT! THERE, THEY HAF **RESPECT**! YAH, **THERE** NOBODY TALKS LIKE THAT TO THE SUPER!
SOON, SOMEDAY WE WILL HAVE DISCIPLINE HERE TOO! YAH, IT'S COMING ...ORDNUNG!

After all, he was the landlord's man—the enemy.
So, between replying to bitter complaints, the nagging and the muttering behind his back, he was left with little else but remoteness to defend his dignity and promote his authority.
MOTHER

His job was
not an easy one.

STOP KNOCKIN' ON THA PIPES, MISSIS FARFELL. I KNOW YOU AIN'T GOT HOT WATER - I JUST STARTED UP THE BOILERS!

JEWS... ALL THE TIME THEY COMPLAIN!

KNOCK KNOCK
GRRR
WHO IS...?

IT'S ME, THE SUPER, MISSIS FARFELL! WOTCHA KNOCKIN' ON THE PIPES FOR??
I AIN'T LETTIN' YOU IN WITH THAT DOG, SCUGGS!

HE WONT HURT NO ONE.
MY NIECE IS TAKIN' A BATH– IN ICE-COLD WATER! YOU WANT SHE SHOULD CATCH NEW-MONIA?
SO, SEND UP HOT WATER.
OK, OK!

AMERICA
ACME COAL · ICE

MOTHER

SSSS
COAL

?
CREAK!
GRRRR

ACME COAL
COMPANY
BEER

TEE...HEE!

?
SLAM
CLICK

YOU WANNA ??

A NICKEL ?

OKAY... OKAY.

FOR A NICKEL JUST ONE LOOK.

THAT'S ENOUGH ...GIMME!

CAN I GIVE YOUR DOG A CANDY?

HERE'S Y'R NICKEL! ...Y'WANNA COME DOWN AGAIN T'MORRA?... I'LL GIVE YA A DIME!

WAIT... LEMME SEE THAT NO ONE IS OUT THERE....

HEY!...YOU TOOK MY MONEY BOX!

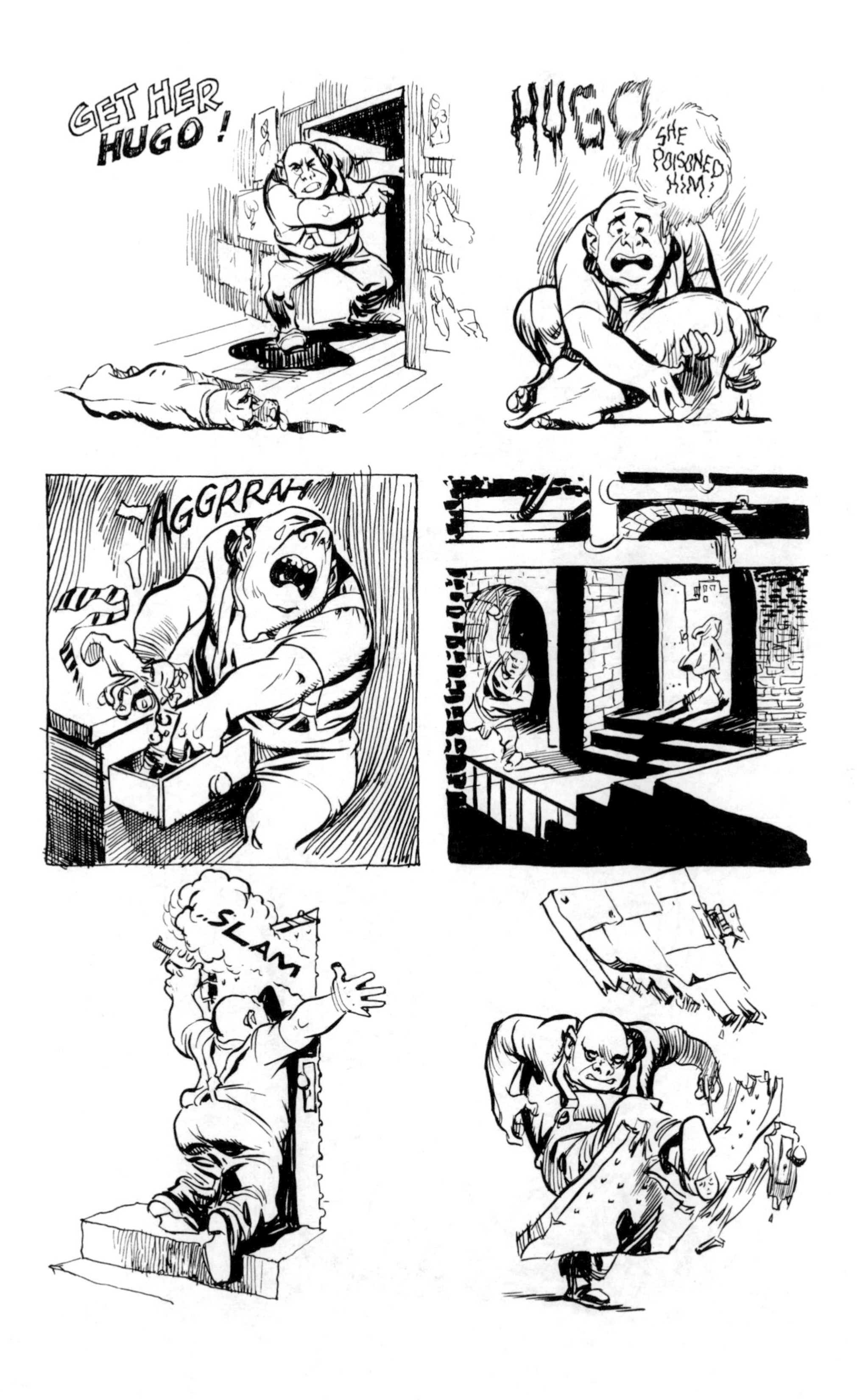
GET HER HUGO!
HUGO
SHE POISONED HIM!
AGGRRAH
SLAM

PUFF
AAGGRR
IF YOU HIT ME... I'LL **TELL** ON YOU!!

ROSIE, WHAT'S GOIN' ON DOWN THERE ?
STEAM HE DON'T SEND UP... BUT LITTLE GOILS - HE BEATS UP!
WHY, THAT'S MR. SCUGGS.
LEGGO THAT KID- YOU - YOU ANIMAL!
HALP... CALL THE POLICE, SOMEBODY, THE SUPER IS KILLIN' ROSIE!!

MURDERER!
ANIMAL!
I NEVER TRUSTED THAT SUPER... HE'S A SEX MANIAC!
DID HE HOIT YOU DOLLINK ?

SLAM
ACME COAL

KNOCK
KNOCK
THIS IS THE POLICE!

OPEN UP SCUGGS THIS IS THE POLICE.
...GO AWAY- OR I SHOOT.
CAREFUL... HE'S GOT A GUN!
NO ONE COMES IN HERE!! THIS IS MY ROOM! I AM THE SUPER HERE!
BREAK IT DOWN FLAHERTY.
STAND BACK EVERYBODY.
BAM!

SOIVES HIM RIGHT-HE NEVER GAVE GOOD STEAM IN WINTER!
WHAT HAPPENED ??
MR. SCUGGS KILLED HIMSELF!!
HE WAS CRAZY ?
WHO KNOWS WHY?
DID HE EVER MOLEST YOUR NIECE ... ER... YOU KNOW, I MEAN... ??
P-L-E-A-S-E OFFICER-NOT IN FRONT OF HER!!! SHE'S ONLY 10 YEARS OLD... OF COURSE NOT!! GOD KNOWS WHAT HE HAD IN MIND?!!

SUPER WANTED
SEE OWNER

SUPER
WANTED

4
RAILROAD

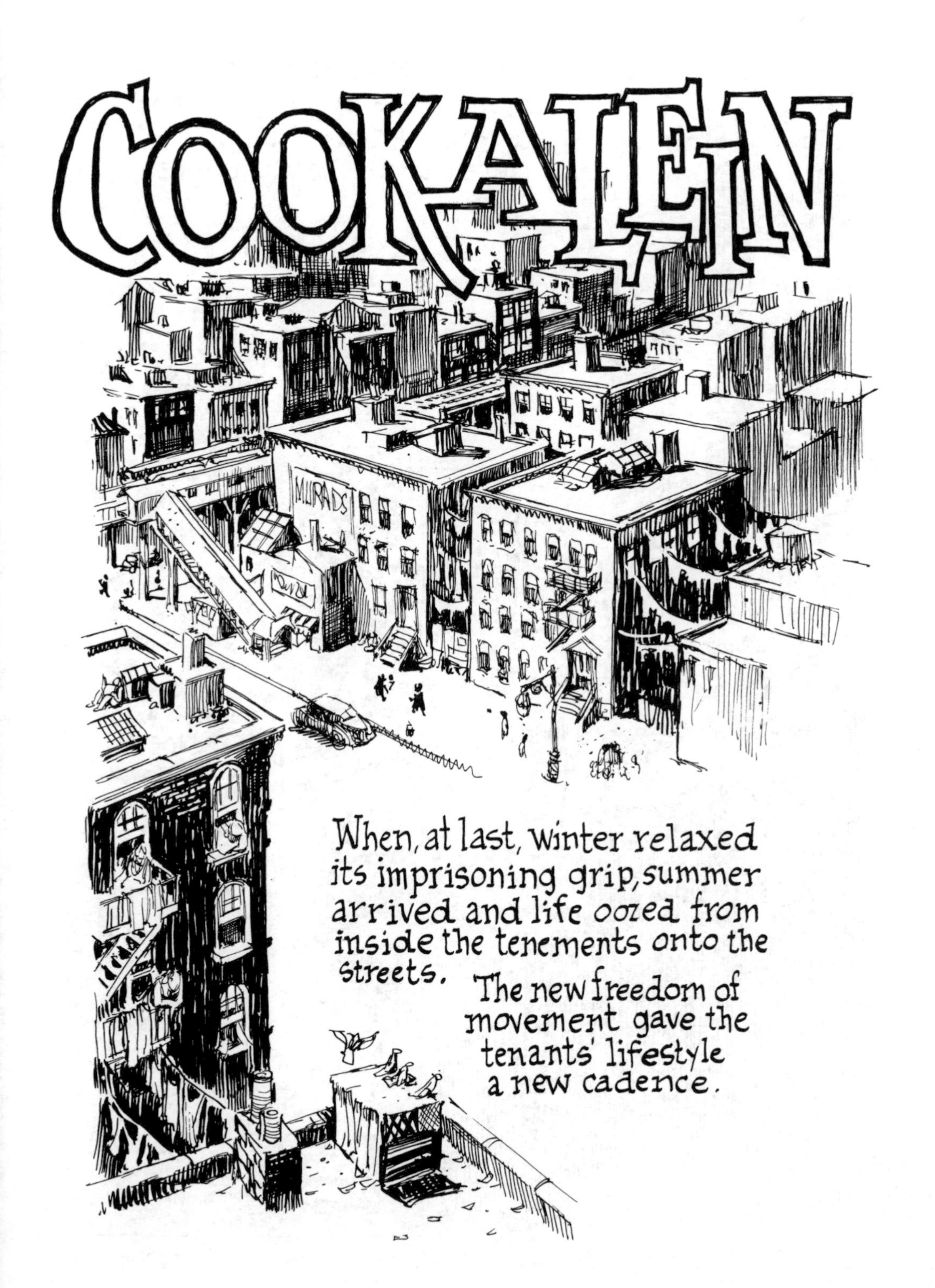
COOKALEIN
MURADS
When, at last, winter relaxed its imprisoning grip, summer arrived and life oozed from inside the tenements onto the streets.
The new freedom of movement gave the tenants' lifestyle a new cadence.

Now communications became easier between the tenants. A new status developed...the vacationers.
YOU GOIN' TO A COOKALEIN AGAIN THIS YEAR, FANNIE?
HAVE I GOT A CHOICE? WE'RE GOIN' TO FEGEL'S FARM UP IN THE MOUNTAINS.

For some tenants it was time to harvest the yield from a year of doing without.

WELL YOU'RE **NOT** GOIN' TO HANG AROUND THE STREETS THIS SUMMER WITH THOSE ROTTEN KIDS!
SO, WHERE WE GOIN', MA?

WE'RE GOIN' TO THE COUNTRY! ...NOW GO TO BED!

HEY, **PA!!** WOT'S A **COOKALEIN??**
IT'S A HOTEL! ... WHERE Y' MOTHER DOES THE COOKING HERSELF!
WE ONLY GET A ROOM TO SLEEP IN... THAT WAY IT'S CHEAPER THAN IN A REG'LAR HOTEL! ...NOW GO TO SLEEP PETEY!

BE PATIENT, FANNIE! NEXT YEAR IF WE HAVE A GOOD SEASON, I'LL START MY OWN LINE!
HAHH!! YOU'LL FAIL LIKE YOU DID BEFORE!! OY, YOU COULD EARN A GOOD LIVING AS A HOUSEPAINTER ...BUT NO-YOU GOTTA BE A FURRIER!

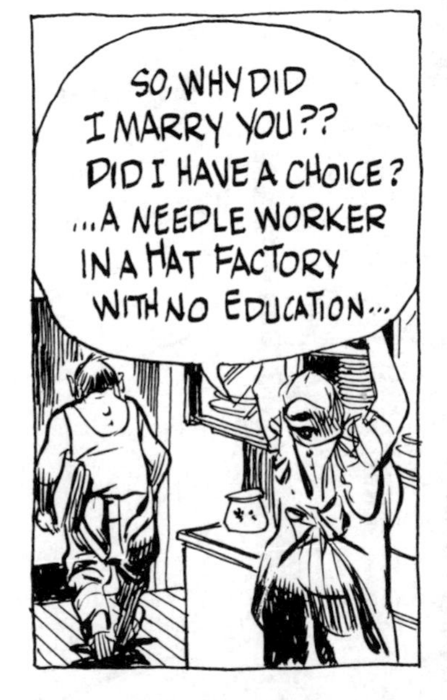
SO, WHY DID I MARRY YOU?? DID I HAVE A CHOICE? ...A NEEDLE WORKER IN A HAT FACTORY WITH NO EDUCATION...

...LIVING LIKE A SLAVE IN MY SISTER'S HOUSE...CLEANING AND WASHING... SO, YOU TOOK ME OUTTA ONE MISERY-INTO ANOTHER!!

ENOUGH, ALREADY! I'VE HEARD IT ALL BEFORE! LET ME SLEEP. TOMORROW I GOT A BIG DAY IN THE SHOWROOM!
HMPF...BIG SHOWROOM MACHER... WHILE YOUR FAMILY HARDLY HAS WHAT TO EAT!

SO, SAM - I HEAR Y'R SENDING FANNIE AND THE KIDS TO THE COUNTRY THIS YEAR!
YEAH, SHE'S GOIN' TO FEGEL'S. IT'S A COOKALEIN.
LA LA MY WIFE'S GONE TO THE COUNTRY HOORAY HOORAY.
SO, NOW WE CAN HAVE TH' PINOCHLE GAME AT YOUR HOUSE, SAM.
PINKUS FURS
SO, GOLDIE... WHEN DO YOU START ON YOUR VACATION?
TOMORROW MORNING! ...BOY, I CAN HARDLY WAIT!

GOLDIE!! DID YOU CALL COHEN ABOUT THAT SKIN SHIPMENT ...I NEED 'EM!
I'M DOIN' IT, MR. PINKUS! I'M DOIN' IT!

SO, GOLDIE, Y' BOUGHT YOUR NEW CLOTHES ALREADY ?
...SPENT ALL MY SAVINGS ON TWO NEW OUTFITS...REAL CLASSY-WITH GOOD LABELS!

THIS YEAR I'M GOING TO GROSSMAN'S-THREE OF MY GIRL-FRIENDS FOUND HUSBANDS UP THERE...I'M GONNA FIND MYSELF A RICH MANUFACTURER!
HOO-BOY F-A-N-C-Y. GONNA COST YOU A PENNY!

HELLO... THIS IS PINKUS FURS - ASK MR. COHEN WHEN WE'RE GONNA GET THE SKINS!?

MR. COHEN- PINKUS WANTS THAT SKIN SHIPMENT!
WOT'S HE NOOjINK ME...?!

It was a time to come to a reckoning with dreams-time to climb over the invisible walls and escape.

BENNY! ARE YOU MESHUGGE? YOU CAN'T AFFORDER A CAR!
HA HA HA I RENTED IT MA... I'M GOIN' TO THE MOUNTAINS IN STYLE.
...A TAXI??? GOLDIE... WHAT'S WRONG WITH THE SUBWAY?
GIRLS WITH CLASS USE A TAXI, MOM!!
TAXI

BOY, WILLIE, LOOKIT THAT NEAT CAR GOIN' DOWN THE BLOCK.
LOOKS LIKE A...A STUDEBAKER OR SOMETHIN'.
COME ON, KIDS, WE'RE LEAVING! ...WE'LL BE LATE, WILLIE!

FANNIE... THIS YEAR TRY TO HAVE A GOOD REST.
IF THE KIDS DON'T GETSICK AND MY ACID CONDITION DON'T START UP... I'LL TRY, SAM... I'LL TRY!! WHO AM I DOING THIS FOR?? THE KIDS!
NU ?? SO WHERE IS THE CATSKILL TRAIN?
WEEHAWKEN
NOT SO LOUD, FANNIE!
TRACK G LADY!
TRAIN G

WEEHAWKEN
I'LL SEE YOU ON THE WEEKEND, FANNIE!
WILLIE...Y'GOT THE SANDWICHES? ..G'BYE, SAM! DON'T MESS UP THE HOUSE!
WILLIE! ...MOVE THE SEAT BACK SO WE CAN SIT TOGETHER.
I'LL DO IT, MA!

HEY, WAVE TO POP... HE LOOKS SAD!
HAH... SOME SAD... NOW HE'S FREE TO HILLYAH AROUND WITH HIS TROMBENIK FRIENDS-BUMS, ALL SUMMER!!!

HMPF... Y'THINK I DON'T KNOW Y'R FATHER... A BIG NOSHER! THE MINIT I'M AWAY HE'S GONNA GRAB A SHIKSEH FROM THE SHOWROOM ... PETEY, SIT STILL - IT'S A LONG TRIP... YOU WANT A BANANA OR SOMETHIN'?

HERE Y'ARE... I'LL TAKE MY BAGS NOW.
THANK YOU MA'AM.
GOOD-BYE FANNIE!
..AHEM...

CAN I HELP YOU?
OH THAT'S SWEET OF YOU... I CAN MANAGE THIS MYSELF THANK YOU!

SEE HOW SHE BRUSHED HIM OFF... VERY CLASSY!
NOT BAD... SHE CAME BY TAXI - MUST BE ONE OF THOSE RICH KIDS FROM WEST END AVENOO!

I'M HAROLD SHMUTZIK, WANNA PLAY CARDS?
SURE, I'M MERSH, PLEASED T'MEETCHA!

Y'GOT THE ROYAL BRUSH OFF! HA, HA, WANNA JOIN US??
SORRY... I'VE GOT SOME READING TO DO!
WHAT ARE YOU... A DOCTOR OR SOMETHIN'?
ALMOST... I'M AN INTERN.
WHERE Y' STAYING?
I'M GOING TO GROSSMAN'S! I'M BLOWIN' A SAX IN THE BAND... IT'S A FREE VACATION AND LOTSA TIME TO STUDY!
I'M WAITING ON TABLES - LOTSA TIPS!
AHH THE TRAIN'S PULLIN' OUT- WE'RE ON TIME.

MOUNTAINVIEW

KUGEL'S MOUNTAIN LODGE!
GROSSMAN'S HOTEL!
O'BRIEN'S HOLLOW, HERE!!
HILLTOP FARMS, HERE!
WILLIE, THERE'S FEGEL'S! ...STAY WITH THE TRUNK, I'LL GET HIM TO HELP LOAD US!
GROSSMANS

SO, MISTER FEGEL...YOU CROWDED THIS SIZZIN?...IS MISSIS FEGEL EXPECTING ME?
YEP!! ALL THE COTTAGES IS TAKEN...YOU GOTTA STAY IN THE MAIN HOUSE.
WELCOME, FANNIE - WE SAVED YOU A BIG ROOM - MY, HOW YOUR KIDS ARE GROWING! WILLIE IS **NOW** OVER 15! ALREADY A MAN, EH?
YES, YES, SO SHOW US THE ROOM, MISSIS FEGEL!

SO, WHERE CAN I PUT MY THINGS MISSIS FEGEL?
WE GIVE YA A CUPBOARD, JUST FOR YOU—THE STOVE, YOU SHARE WITH THE OTHER LADIES...
I START COOKIN' EARLY.
WELCOME
HEY...WHAT'S NEW THIS YEAR AROUND HERE MR. FEGEL??
WAL...THIS YEAR WE GOT ENTERTAINMENT ...I BUILT A CASINO OUTTA THE OLD BARN...Y'CAN DANCE WITH THE OLD LADIES..HAHA...SO, WE AIN'T GROSSMAN'S!

GROSSMAN'S
ABE & JENNIE GROSSMAN
Proprietors
GROSSMAN'S

WELCOME TO GROSSMAN'S
H'YA FOLKS...WELCOME TO GROSSMAN'S HAHA
DANNY, YOU HERE AGAIN THIS YEAR?
DANNY, THE TUMMLER, IS NOW THE SOCIAL DIRECTOR.
ACTIVITY ♫ ACTIVITY ♫ LOTSA ACTION... ...TANGO LESSONS AT THREE – MISSIS GOLDFARB!
OY... WHAT A DEVIL!

GET SETTLED KIDS! AFTER SUPPER WE GOT WHOOPIE IN THE CASINO! SEE YOU LATER!

...AHEM! HI, GOLDIE.

ER... AHEM... S-SURE IS A... A BEAUTIFUL NIGHT.
HOW DO YOU KNOW MY NAME?

...LOOKED IT UP IN THE HOTEL'S REGISTER ...MINE'S **HERBIE**, WE MET ON THE TRAIN!

REALLY?

LOOK, SINCE I EAT WITH THE HELP– I WON'T BE IN THE DINING ROOM WITH YOU... SO, MAYBE LATER–AFTER THE DANCING, WE COULD HAVE A SODA, OR...
OH, SO YOU'RE ONE OF THE HELP? ...WELL...ER, I'M SORRY, I'LL BE-ER-BUSY!! YES, I GOT TO WASH MY HAIR!

AW, COME ON... WHAT'S WRONG WITH ME?
OH, IT'S NOT **YOU**... IT'S JUST- WELL... I MEAN SOCIALLY WE'RE NOT EQUAL. I DIDN'T COME UP HERE JUST TO MEET A-A SAXOPHONE PLAYER!

LOOK... YOU'RE A NICE BOY- LOTSA NICE WAITRESSES OR CHAMBERMAIDS WOULD LOVE TO MEET YOU...
OKAY-HAVE IT YOUR WAY-SEE YA AROUND!

HEY, LOOKA THE NEW ARRIVAL!
MUST BE A RICH MANUFACTURER ... A 'CLOAKIE'... LOOKA THAT NEAT CAR... HOO HA!
HONK
HONK

BOY... TAKE MY BAGS AND PARK MY CAR ...HA.. BOY, I MADE IT FROM THE BRONX IN 5 HOURS!
HERE!
WOW$$
WHICH WAY IS THE DESK??
THAT WAY!
THANKS... SEE YOU LATER BABY!
SURE.
LEMME RING THE COWBELL TOO, JOEY!
DINNER TIME EVVYBODY!
CLANG

HEY, SHLOIM! WAITING TABLES AGAIN THIS YEAR?
-YEH IT COULD BE WOISE!
HELLO SHERL.
WHO YOU SITTING WITH THIS YEAR?
AHH MISSIS GOLD_ _I GOT FOR YOU THE SAME TABLE FROM LAST YEAR...
OKAY, POP, WHERE IS THE ACTION??
VELL ... I'LL TELLYOU... THAT GOIL ON TABLE 6 OOH, HOO L-O-A-D-E-D... HER FATHER IS IN DIAMONDS ... BUT SHE'S UP HERE WIT A NOSY AUNT!
6
ALSO... WE GOT ON TABLE 8... A BEAUTY, ...RICH... I HEAR SHE'S FROM THE DRESS BUSINESS...
HMM... I'LL TAKE TABLE 8 - SEAT ME THERE!
8
SO, O.K. ...VOT'S YOUR LINE?
I'M IN FURS ...BENNY BAUM...! BUT KEEP IT ONNA Q.T. -LOTSA GOLD DIGGERS, Y'KNOW!

STOP SINGING ABE, AND DILL THE CODDS...OY, BOYCHIK, I'M TELLINK YOU, IT'S A MECHAYE... A WHOLE MONTH WE CAN PLAY PINOCHLE WIT NO WIMMEN TO BODDER US!
MY WIFE WENT TO THE COUNTRY HOORAY HOORAY
SAM, DO ME A FAVOR AND CLOSE THE WINDER...C'MON ...PAY ATTENTION TO THE GAME!

ER... JUST GETTIN' SOME AIR!
SAM... C'MON, YOU GONNA PLAY CODDS-UDDER YA GONNA LOOK OUT TH' WINDER?

SAM!...VERE YOU GOIN'?... IT'S YORE PARTY-SO, SIT ALREADY!
PLAY, PLAY...BE MY GUEST... ER-I GOTTA VISIT MY TANTE MINNIE...SHE GOT AN ATTACK TODAY...SUDDENLY...

KATHLEEN

SAM HONEY!

CHRIST, SAM, YOU AIN'T BEEN AROUND SINCE EASTER!

DON'T WORRY. WE GOT A MONTH TOGETHER!

MY WIFE'S GONE TO THE COUNTRY!

LISSEN, HONEY-IT'S THREE YEARS WE BEEN LIKE THIS...WHEN ARE WE GONNA DO SOMETHIN' ABOUT IT??
ABOUT WHAT? YOU KNOW I GOT TWO KIDS, KATHLEEN!!

AND WHAT DO I HAVE?? SAM, LEAVE YOUR WIFE...TELL HER THIS WEEKEND!
OY, VEY... IT'LL KILL HER...SHE AIN'T A WELL WOMAN.

SAM...IT'S GETTIN' LATE FOR ME...WE AIN'T NO CHICKENS, Y'KNOW!
OKAY, OKAY-SO, I'LL TELL HER WHEN I GO UP ON FRIDAY!

ACME COATS
SHOWROOM
IRVING... I HEAR YOUR WIFE IS 'HILLYINK' UP IN THE MOUNTAINS!!
HA HA HA
HOW DID YOU FIND OUT??
OH, WOID GETS AROUND... WANT MY ADVICE??... DROP IN ON HER THIS WEEKEND ...AKSEDENTAL...
HELLO, SAM... IRVING MINKS, Y'GOT ROOM IN THE CAR? I'M COMIN' UP TO THE MOUNTAINS THIS WEEKEND!... THANKS!
HEY, SAM!... YOU GOT ROOM IN THE CAR FRIDAY?
NO!... I JUST PROMISED A SPACE TO IRVING MINKS... THAT FILLS IT UP... SORRY, I DON'T WANT TO OVERLOAD-IT'S MY BROTHER'S CAR!

...LISSEN, SAM, DROP ME OFF AT GROSSMAN'S...ER I'LL COME UP TO FEGEL'S COOKALEIN LATER! ...ER DON'T TELL ANYONE I'M COMING, O.K?
SURE, IRVING! Y'GONNA SURPRISE MISSIS MINKS ?
YEAH!

NOW, WILLIE...POPPA'S COMING UP TONIGHT-SO YOU SLEEP IN THE BARN...PETEY, YOU'RE GOING DOWN TO GROSSMAN'S TO STAY WITH AUNT ROSE..YIZZLE SLEEP WITH YOUR COUSIN!
OKAY!
AWW WISHT I COULD SLEEP IN THE BARN TOO !!

HELLO, FANNIE!
SAM!!... JUST IN TIME FOR SUPPER ...WASH UP AND COME TO THE KITCHEN!
SO SAM, HOW'S IN THE CITY??
HOT,
SO, HOW COME **YOUR** HUSBAND NEVER COMES UP, MISSIS MINKS?
HE'S ON THE ROADA LOT! HE'S A SALESMAN, Y'KNOW!
TONIGHT WE ARE HAVING A DANCE IN THE CASINO --IN HONOR OF THE HUSBANDS!
HOO, HOO LOOK IT OUR WILLIE DANCING WITH MISSIS MINKS... A **MAN** ALREADY!
HFF... SHE SHOULD KEEP HER HANDS OFF HIM... HE'S ONLY 15!

AHEM... IT'S GETTIN' LATE... W-I-L-L-IE!
HMM♫ WILLIE, YOU ARE A VERY GOOD DANCER...ER.. HOW OLD ARE YOU?
ER... AH.. 19..AH GOIN' ON 20, MISSIS MINKS.
GOOD NIGHT LADIES
GOOD NIGHT, MISSIS FARFEL.
THAT WAS A NICE DANCE.
GOOD NIGHT!
GOOD NIGHT!
WHERE'S WILLIE, FANNIE ??
HE'S GONNA SLEEP IN THE BARN. C'MON UP TO BED, SAM!

FANNIE...
STOP, SAM...THE WALLS ARE PAPER-THIN.

SO..?? WE'RE MAN AND WIFE...AIN'T WE??
HA...SOME MAN AND WIFE! YOU THINK I DONT KNOW ABOUT YOUR SHIKSEH??

MAYBE IF YOU WAS MORE INTERESTED IN SEX!!
SHHAH, DON'T USE DIRTY WORDS!

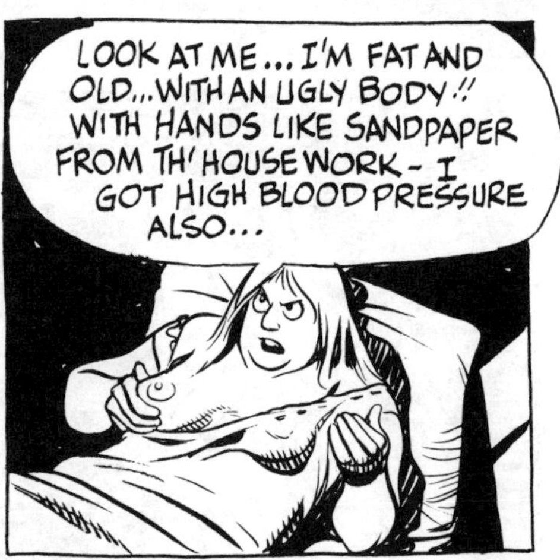
LOOK AT ME...I'M FAT AND OLD...WITH AN UGLY BODY!! WITH HANDS LIKE SANDPAPER FROM TH' HOUSEWORK - I GOT HIGH BLOOD PRESSURE ALSO...

SO WHAT DO WE DO?? A DIVORCE?
I AINT GIVING YOU NO DIVORCE! WE GOT KIDS TO THINK OF - YOU WANNA PLAY AROUND WITH YOUR SHIKSEH??..GO!! I'LL HIDE IT FROM THE KIDS SO THEY WONT BE ASHAMED!

OH FANNIE THIS IS NO LIFE TOGETHER...
...LISSEN SAM-IF YOU WERE A BETTER PROVIDER THEN YOU COULD HAVE A BETTER LIFE WITH ME...

PSST WILLIE...
M. MISSIS MINKS...

I BROUGHT YOU A BLANKET, WILLIE, IN CASE YOU WERE COLD...
TH-THANK Y-YOU
...SURE IS NICE OF YOU, MISSIS MINKS!
CALL ME MARALYN ... BRRRRR NOW...I'M COLD!
YOU GONNA INVITE ME IN?
GULP ER, YES, SURE!
MMMMM TEE HEE I CAN FEEL YOUR YOU-KNOW-WHAT GETTING BIG ...AHHH
YOU SMELL SO NICE.
WILLIE DARLING...AHHH NOW, NOW...NOW... DO IT!... DO-IT-TO-ME

AHHH HOW OLD ARE YOU REALLY, WILLIE?
GEE, MARALYN... GUESS I CAME TOO FAST...SORRY... I, I'M ONLY 15 !!

NAH, SWEETIE...THAT WAS PRETTY MANLY FOR SOMEONE YOUR AGE...I'M GOING TO TEACH YOU...BY THE END OF THE SUMMER YOU'LL BE...

EEK OH MY GOD!!

SO,...I MIGHTA KNOWN...MY MARALYN IN THE HAY WITH A KID!! HA!
IRVING! HOW...WHEN DID YOU GET HERE?!

I HEARD YOU WERE UP TO YOUR OLD TRICKS ...SO, I CAME UP TO FIND OUT... HA! SOME-ONE IN THE HOUSE SAW YOU GO INTO THE BARN-AT THIS TIME OF NIGHT??...HA! I FIGGERED OUT THE REST!
IRVING! I WAS JUST COMING TO GET SOME FRESH MILK AND THIS KID PROPOSITIONS ME... HAHAHA IMAGINE, HE'S ONLY 15!
LIAR
IRVING NO! NO!

WOTSAMATTER ?!
I'M NOT ENOUGH
FOR YOU??

IRVING,
DARLING...
P-L-E-A-S-E
YOU KNOW
HOW I AM...
HOW I NEED!

OKAY...SO
YOU'LL DO IT
WITH ME!
YES, YES...
LET ME TAKE
YOUR PANTS
OFF...OH, IRVING
YOU'RE SO..SO
SEXY...

OOOOH..YESS, YESS..
DARLING OOOOHHHHH
AHHHHH I LOVE IT...
I..R..V..I..N..G...

OOHHH... IRVING, DARLING- THAT WAS WONDERFUL.
C'MON... WE'RE GOIN' UP TO YOUR ROOM!
...NO KIDDIN'?? ...AND HE'S ONLY 15?!! WOW.... HA HA HA HA

GEE HILDIE... IT IS PRETTY CLASSY HERE AT GROSSMAN'S!
HOW COME YOUR FOLKS SENT YOU DOWN HERE TO SLEEP WITH US, PETEY??
'CAUSE POPPA CAME UP—AND THERE WAS NO ROOM FOR ME.
YOUR MA AND PA WANNA SLEEP TOGETHER -YOU KNOW WHY?
TO TALK PRIVATE... OR MAYBE TO FIGHT_ I DUNNO!

DUMBELL !! YOU DON'T KNOW NUTHIN!... HEE, HEE, HEE, HEE, HEE !!
HEY !! LEGGO! THAT'S MY PEEPEE, HILDA !

Y' WANNA FEEL MINE? GO ON!
YEA, HAW YOU AIN'T GOT ONE! IT'S JUST A HOLE!

YOU MEAN YOU CAN PEE OUTTA THAT HOLE? GOSH!
DUMBELL !! GIRLS ARE DIFFERENT!

HSST...PETEY... WANNA WATCH THE GROWN-UPS DOIN' DIRTY THINGS?
YEAHHH,...IF WE WON'T GET INTER TROUBLE!

SHHH DON'T MAKE NOISE AND COME WITH ME...
SHH
THERE...Y'SEE??
WOW
PLEASE... BENNY... NOT LIKE THIS... I WANT YOU SHOULD RESPECT ME!
GOLDIE... GOLDIE! WE'RE GONNA GET MARRIED... SO WHY NOT DO IT NOW... I'M PROPOSIN', GOLDIE!!

OKAY... OKAY.!! SO, WE'LL WAIT UNTIL WE'RE MARRIED... BUT HONEY, LET'S DO IT RIGHT AWAY! THIS PLACE IS COSTING ME A PRETTY PENNY!
?
BUT BENNY, I THOUGHT YOU WERE ...I MEAN, YOU'RE A RICH... THAT IS, YOU **ARE** A MANUFACTURER AREN'T YOU??
WELL, TO TELL THE TRUTH GOLDIE, **I'M NOT**... I'M JUST A CUTTER! OH, WELL, SO YOUR FOLKS'LL TAKE ME INTO THE BUSINESS! AFTER WE'RE MARRIED WHAT'S THE DIFFERENCE?!

OH, NO!! HA HA HA HA IT'S A RIOT!! OH, BENNY BENNY....
WHAT'S SO FUNNY ?
I'M NOT RICH EITHER... MY FOLKS ARE POOR, THEY CAN HARDLY SUPPORT ME!
YOU'RE NOT ??! ?
BENNY... IF YOU LOVE ME - NOTHING ELSE MATTERS! IT DOESN'T MAKE A DIFFERENCE! ...YOU EARN A GOOD LIVING, DON'T YOU!?

SAY SOMETHING, BENNY!

WHAT ARE YOU DOING BENNY !!?

BENNY.. ...NO! NO NO
I'M A GOOD GIRL!
IT'S AWHOLE NEW BALLGAME NOW BABY!

NO STOP!

SEE... WHAT'D I TELL YOU!! C'MON LET'S GET OUTTA HERE!!
WOWEE!!
BENNY BEN...
OH MY GOD OH MY GOD!
OH MY GOD OH MY GOD!
GOLDIE, WHAT HAPPENED TO YOU!?

HE RAPED ME...OH, MY GOD!
SHH... IT'S OKAY NOW GOLDIE!

GET A DOCTOR.
I'M A DOCTOR ...I KNOW WHAT TO DO!

YOU'LL BE OKAY...
OOOH.. I'M A RUINED WOMAN!! MY GOD... A TRAMP... A WHORE! WHO WILL WANT ME AFTER THIS!? OH MY GOD...

I'LL HAVE YOU GOLDIE... I LOVE YOU... IT DOESN'T MATTER TO ME WHETHER YOU'RE A VIRGIN OR NOT... IT'S **YOU** I WANT!
SNFF **YOU**??.. Y-YOU'RE HERBIE... WE MET ON THE TRAIN... LATER I SNUBBED YOU... I-I'M SO ASHAMED... HERBIE!

...YOU REST NOW, GOLDIE! NO ONE NEED EVER KNOW -NOT EVEN YOUR PARENTS! IN A MONTH OR TWO, I'LL BE GOING INTO PRIVATE PRACTICE. WE'LL GET MARRIED-AND THAT'S THAT!!

GET SOME SLEEP... I GOTTA PLAY WITH THE BAND - IT'S MY JOB!

HERBIE!

YES?

I LIKE YOU... VERY MUCH!

SO, YOU'RE RUTHIE FEIN, THE HEIRESS.
OH, **BENNIE**, I HOPE YOU WON'T LET MY FATHER'S WEALTH COME BETWEEN US!

BENNY!

YEAH?? OH, HO... IT'S HERBIE THE TRUMPETER! ...LOOK, I'M BUSY...
YOU MIGHT LIKE TO KNOW THAT GOLDIE IS O.K. BENNY!

SO?? HA!!... THAT PHONEY T'MATER! A CHEAP SECRETARY ...A NICE BODY THO'.
YOU DON'T GET IT, BENNY!

YOU DIDN'T EVEN PENETRATE... YOU ARE SICK, BENNY... I MEAN, SEXUALLY... YOU NEED MEDICAL HELP... DO YOU UNDERSTAND?

HOW DO YOU KNOW...?! I MEAN, HOW DID YOU KNOW THAT ABOUT ME??
I'M A DOCTOR, BENNY, BELIEVE ME, I KNOW!
WHY DON'T WE BOTH KEEP QUIET ABOUT THIS!... DON'T EVER MENTION GOLDIE'S NAME... EVER!
O.K. O.K.
WHAT WAS THAT ABOUT, BENNY?
OH, ER.. SOME GUY WANTS ADVICE ABOUT HIS GIRL!
OH, BENNY, YOU MUST BE A HEE HEE DEVIL WITH GIRLS... YOU'RE SO SOPHISTICATED!
YEH... SO, WHEN AM I GONNA MEET YOUR FOLKS??

And so the summer ends... and like migratory birds the vacationers return to the sanctuary of the tenement where normal life resumes.

SO, GOLDIE, YOU HAD A GOOD VACATION ??
YEAH...I MET A DOCTOR ...WE'RE GETTING MARRIED IN TWO MONTHS!
MAZEL TOV!
WELL, BENNY, BACK FROM THE MOUNTAINS?! SO, HOW WAS IT??
GREAT! I'M QUITTING THIS JOB!! I'M MARRYING A GIRL I MET- HER FATHER IS TAKING ME INTO THE DIAMOND BUSINESS!

NU...WILLIE? VACATION'S OVER ALREADY! SO, START GETTING READY FOR SCHOOL!! THIS YEAR YOU'RE GONNA HAVE LOTSA RESPONSIBILITY AROUND HERE...YOUR FATHER IS.... ...GONNA BE AH TRAVELLING ALOT...SO, YIZZEL BE THE MAN OF THE HOUSE NOW!...Y'HEAR ME WILLIE...WILLIE?

About the Author

Will Eisner (1917–2005) was present at the birth of the comic book industry in the 1930s, creating such titles as *Blackhawk* and *Sheena, Queen of the Jungle*. He created *The Spirit* in 1940, syndicating it for twelve years as a unique and innovative sixteen-page Sunday newspaper insert, with a weekly circulation of 5 million copies. As a Pentagon-based warrant officer during World War II, Eisner pioneered the instructional use of comics, continuing to produce them for the U.S. Army under civilian contract into the 1970s, along with educational comics for clients as diverse as General Motors and elementary school children.

In 1978 Eisner created *A Contract With God*, launching a bold new literary genre. Nearly twenty celebrated graphic novels followed, affirming his position as the grand old man of comics. Since 1988 the comic industry's top awards for excellence have been called "The Eisners." Throughout his career, Eisner received numerous honors and awards worldwide, including only the second Lifetime Achievement Award bestowed by the National Foundation for Jewish Culture (2002). In 2005, as one of his final projects, Eisner created *The Contract With God Trilogy*, which combined three of his great semiautobiographical novels all set on the mythical Dropsie Avenue in the Bronx—*A Contract With God*, *A Life Force*, and *Dropsie Avenue*. Michael Chabon's Pulitzer Prize–winning novel *The Amazing Adventures of Kavalier & Clay* is based in good part on Eisner.

Also available from the Will Eisner Library

Called "a masterpiece" by R. Crumb, *A Life Force* chronicles not only the Great Depression but also the rise of Nazism and spread of socialist politics, through the depiction of his protagonist, Jacob Shtarkah, whose existential search reflected Eisner's own lifelong struggle.

ISBN: 978-0-393-32803-5
Price: $16.95
150 pages

In ***Dropsie Avenue: The Neighborhood***, Eisner graphically traces the social trajectory of this mythic avenue over four centuries, creating a sweeping panorama of the city and its waves of new residents, whose stories present an unending "story of life, death, and resurrection."

ISBN: 978-0-393-32811-0
Price: $16.95
186 pages